INVESTING FOR BEGINNERS

A COMPLETE GUIDE TO MASTERING BITCOIN, CRYPTOCURRENCY INVESTING, INITIAL COIN OFFERING, MINING AND TRADING

ROBERT EATON

COPYRIGHT

CONTENTS

Introduction   v

1. INVESTING 101: THE BASICS   1
2. YOUR INVESTMENT OPTIONS   4
3. CREATING A WINNING INVESTING PLAN   14
4. UNDERSTANDING & MITIGATING RISK   18
5. DIVERSIFICATION & ASSET ALLOCATION   23
6. CALCULATING RETURNS ON INVESTMENTS   27
7. SMART INVESTMENT SELECTION   38
8. MANAGING YOUR INVESTMENT PORTFOLIO   41
9. BENEFITS OF INVESTING   46
10. TIPS FROM THE GREATS   49
11. QUICK START GUIDE   52
12. CONCLUSION   54

INTRODUCTION

Considering the famous saying that 'money doesn't grow on trees', it's remarkable how rich you can become through the information available in books.

This two-book bundle guide will be instrumental in offering the information required for you to begin your investment or trading journey.

First we will explore the basics of investing and create a roadmap for an absolute beginner to follow to success.

With a little bit of guidance anyone can become a successful investor, it is simply a matter of preparation.

If you are a newbie thinking of diving into the markets then consider this book your first real investment.

You won't find complicated strategies or schemes here. Before any of that you need to lay a solid foundation, and that is exactly what this book will achieve.

Before you place any money on the line you owe it to yourself to understand what you are getting into. This book will teach you, step-by-step, the absolute essentials.

INTRODUCTION

By the time you have finished reading you will be ready to decide which road to go down and, under my professional guidance, we'll get you heading straight for success!

Let's get started.

INVESTING 101: THE BASICS

Saving to meet the down payment on a new car or home is different from investing to achieve the same goal. So, what exactly does it mean to be an investor?

Most people believe that investing is using money to make more money. While this notion is true, savvy investors aim to accomplish more than just making money with their investments.

According to Benjamin Graham's book, 'The Intelligent Investor', an investment operation is one that, through analysis, promises safety of invested capital and satisfactory capital gains.

Quite simply put, investing, by definition, is the act of risking money or any other form of wealth to earn a return in the future. However it is not, at least as covered in this guide, the same as saving.

SAVING VERSUS INVESTING

Saving involves holding money in a bank account, money market, building society or any other account that is relatively safe. Such saving plans earn interest, albeit low.

An alternative way to save is through a money market fund, which invests in short-term investments such as treasury bills issued by governments. The funds are relatively liquid, and therefore it is fairly easy for you to access your money.

Don't worry if you aren't grasping some of the terminology just jet, all will become clear in the forthcoming chapters.

Savings, then, do not earn as much return as investments do. Consequently, the value of savings may be eroded by the purchasing power of the respective currency and inflation in the long run.

Investments, on the other hand, involve taking greater risks than savings, and hence present an opportunity to earn higher returns.

Due to the higher level of risk undertaken, it is important to understand that the value of investments may also decline, or the investor may suffer a total loss of the entire investment, also known as 'losing the principle investment.'

This principle goes hand in hand with the saying, 'the higher the risk; the higher the return.' This will be covered later under risk management.

The goals set for saving are also different from those of investing. Most savers view savings as money set aside in case of a rainy day. Such funds should be kept safe from any risk of loss since they could be needed at a moment's notice.

The majority of savers who are not aware of the available investment opportunities end up saving too large a portion of their disposable income, when they could instead be putting it to work for them.

It is important to note that investors save, too. This is crucial because sometimes funds are needed to cover emergency spending and should be stored in a place that is easily accessible.

Typically, investors make savings to cover personal expenses, utility bills, clothing and food for the unforeseeable future.

Most newbie investors look to accrue wealth in a short timeframe and hence do not give much weight to savings. Unless you come from a wealthy background, saving money by living within your means is crucial to the wellbeing of your investment life and generation of wealth.

So, the savings ingredient in investing provides enough stability to allow you to take care of pressing needs without drawing from your investments. It is advisable for everyone to save a little portion of funds every time a paycheck or other income is received.

To summarize, savings and investments should not be treated the same way given that each of them serves a different purpose. Every knowledgeable investor and saver should assess his or her financial goals as well as obligations for both the short and long-term timeframe and decide on the amount of investments and savings to make. Savings should be compared more to a form of insurance and not be confused with investments.

CHAPTER SUMMARY

- People invest to preserve and generate more wealth, while they save to create capital for investment and/or emergencies.
- While savings earn low interests, they are relatively low-risk since regulated monetary authorities usually back them.
- Investments have a relatively higher rate of return compared to savings, but involve greater risk.
- Funds saved are easier to access than those invested.
- Saving is a prerequisite of investing.

YOUR INVESTMENT OPTIONS

One of the major dilemmas that new and potential investors face is regarding what type of investments to make.

Many people are unaware of the different investment instruments available, while those in the know are often overwhelmed by the varieties available.

Investment, as derived from its definition in the previous chapter, comprises of two key features: the promise of reward and the inherent risk that comes with this promise.

An investment, also referred to as a security or asset elsewhere in this book, can be classified in two broad categories: marketable and non-marketable.

NON-MARKETABLE ASSETS

Don't be misled by the name, non-marketable securities are named so, not because they cannot be sold or bought, but because they don't trade like shares on a normal securities exchange.

Instead, they can be bought or sold in a private transaction in the exchange market in a process known as an 'over the counter' transaction. However, some non-marketable securities are extremely personal and cannot be sold.

Characteristics of non-marketable investments:

- The parties involved in this kind of investment are usually an institution and an investor.
- Are untradeable but liquid. Though they can be turned into cash, it is not always easy as sometimes this process comes at a cost. For instance, in the case of a savings account, a defaulting fee may apply.
- These securities are personal in nature. When changing hands, both sides must know each other; consequently, the investor must table his documents to reveal his identity.
- Nonmarketable securities are low-risk investments, since the institutions that issue them are often insured, the chances of the issuer defaulting is extremely low.

Examples of non-marketable investments:

SAVINGS ACCOUNT

This is a standard deposit account that earns interest. The higher the amount deposited, the higher the rate of return. Sometimes withdrawals are allowed, but with notice. Savings accounts are offered by financial institutions such as banks, credit unions, and societies.

GOVERNMENT SAVINGS BONDS

Are non-traded government debt. (Learn about bonds in the subsequent sections).

NON-NEGOTIABLE CERTIFICATES OF DEPOSITS (CD)

A CD is a savings certificate issued by commercial banks to a depositor that entitles him or her to receive a specified interest over a stated period. CDs are low-risk investments as they are insured. In layman terms, this is a preconditioned loan from an individual to a bank, with interest as the reward.

MONEY MARKET DEPOSIT ACCOUNT

This is a deposit account with limited withdrawals that earns higher interest (the prevailing rate in the money market) than a conventional savings account.

As you can see, non-marketable assets play an integral part in investment. They can be used as a prerequisite to investing.

MARKETABLE ASSETS

Marketable assets are those that can easily be exchanged for money. An investor with such investments can sell them any moment he wishes to, since most of them trade in a well-established market.

There are four classes of marketable investments, as below:

- Money market securities
- Capital market investments
- Derivatives
- Investment funds

Let's look them over one by one.

MONEY MARKET SECURITIES

Money market securities are short-term debt instruments with a redemption period limit not exceeding 12 months, offered by governments and corporations in need of funding.

Characteristics of money market instruments:

- The maturity period does not exceed 12 months.
- They have a minimum transaction limit, typically not less than $100,000.

- Are easily exchangeable for cash since they earn fixed-income within a short period.
- They are low-risk investments since the issuer must have a high credit rating, so there is minimal chance of defaulting.
- Marketable securities are offered at a discount of their face value.

Examples of money market instruments:

T-BILLS

These are risk-free assets sold by governments to raise funds and dictate the interest rates in the market. An increase in the supply of treasury bills leads to an increase in the interest rates, while reducing the supply cuts the rates. T-bills may have a maturity period of three, six or nine months. They are sold in weekly auctions and have a specified face value, which is paid to the holder on maturity.

COMMERCIAL PAPERS

An unsecured, short-term debt instrument issued by a corporation to finance short-term liabilities, inventories, and accounts receivable. Maturity period of such an asset is seldom longer than 270 days.

NEGOTIABLE CERTIFICATE OF DEPOSITS

Are tradable promissory notes offered by commercial banks to their depositors who are then entitled to a specified interest until maturity. Unlike the previous two examples, there are CDs available under $100,000.

BANK ACCEPTANCE

Are similar to treasury bills, save for the fact that they are issued by nonfinancial firms guaranteed by a bank. They are redeemable within one month or three months.

REPURCHASE AGREEMENTS (REPO)

Is short-term borrowing for dealers in government securities, such as bonds and T-bills. A holder of such securities may sell them to an investor, with an agreement to buy them back the next day. This agreement is what is called a REPO. The maturity here is 24 hours.

EURODOLLAR BONDS

This is a dollar-dominated bond issued by conglomerates or governments, with the money raised being held in a foreign institution, not the home of the issuer or the USA. Holding far from the jurisdiction of the regulatory body helps minimize costs. The parties involved are limited to large institutions since the minimum deposit is huge and the maturity is short-term, usually less than six months. However, individuals can invest indirectly in this market through money market funds (more on that later).

CAPITAL MARKET INVESTMENTS

Capital markets offer the platform for companies, institutions, and governments to raise funds from individuals willing to generate wealth through instruments, such as shares and long-term loans.

Capital market investments are therefore investment products with a maturity period normally ranging from a year to perpetuity. They are classified in two broad categories, as follows:

- Fixed income
- Equities/Stocks

FIXED INCOME SECURITIES (BONDS)

Fixed income securities are issued by governments or corporations to raise funds through debt instruments.

The investors, in this case, the holders of such instruments, are entitled to returns in terms of fixed periodic payments and later the principal amount at maturity. However, there is a type of bond known as the zero-coupon that doesn't pay periodically, but makes a lump sum payment, often the par value, at maturity.

The issuer (corporation or government) can be put into bankruptcy by the bondholder should it default on payment.

Types of bonds:

CORPORATE BONDS

Debt instruments issued by corporations.

TREASURY BONDS/NOTES

Are issued by governments and have a maturity of at least year but no more than ten years.

MUNICIPAL BONDS

Are debt instruments offered by lower units of the government to fund their projects. Such units include states, counties, cities, townships, etc.

FEDERAL AGENCY BONDS

Some public bodies have the independence to finance their operations and may opt to raise funds through the bond market. The government guarantees these bonds.

EQUITIES/STOCKS

Stocks represent a part ownership of a company, and are arguably the most favored form of investing. Investors who buy shares or stocks of a particular company are referred to as shareholders of that company. Their returns are based on the growth and revenues of the company as well as the value of the stock.

There are two types of stocks, preferential and common stocks. To learn more, pick up my beginner's guide to stocks on Amazon by searching 'Rich Harrington Stocks'.

DERIVATIVES/CONTINGENT CLAIMS

Besides the two types of marketable securities already discussed, money market and capital market securities, there are the derivatives.

The name is descriptive in nature; derivatives are securities that derive their value from the underlying basket of assets.

Such securities include futures and options, and rights and warrants.

OPTIONS

An option is a right to buy a particular investment instrument at a specified price and time in the future. The right to buy is referred to as the 'call' option, while that to sell is the 'put' option. Options are available for commodities, stocks, and currencies.

Investors can opt out of the investment at the future date if they find it unfavorable, only paying a fixed premium fee.

FUTURES

An investor who invests in futures gets returns when the future prices of the selected commodities are as he or she expected. A future is an obligation to buy or sell a certain amount of commodity at a set price at a specific date in future.

For instance, an investor can purchase a commodity future; let's say soya bean futures, at a fixed price now, to be delivered at a particular future date. If the price of the soya beans at that specific future date is greater than the fixed price he bought at, he can sell the soya beans at the market price, gaining a return on investment. Apart from commodities, futures also exist for stocks, bonds, and currencies.

Options and futures differ in the fact that options represent a right, while futures are an obligation.

RIGHTS AND WARRANTS

A publicly traded firm may wish to raise funds by offering its shares, but doing so publicly may dilute the price of the stock. Such a firm employs rights and/or warrants to execute this plan.

• Rights enable shareholders to buy shares of their firm at a predetermined price (often lower the current market price) in proportion to the shares they already own.

• Warrants entitle the holder to buy the underlying stock of the issuer at a specified price (exercise price) before the expiration of the preset period. They are quite similar to options as they are both contractual agreements giving the holder rights to buy a given security, but warrants are issued by corporations, while options are contracts between investors.

INVESTMENT FUNDS (MUTUAL FUNDS)

As a rookie investor, the choices covered above may overwhelm you, or you may be too busy to study the different investment options available. Don't worry if that is the case, you needn't feel locked out, for the following is a fantastic option for you.

Investment funds are indirect investments undertaken through investing in an investment firm. These mutual funds are professionally managed, and invested in different securities on behalf of their shareholders.

Types of investment funds:

HEDGE FUNDS

Are aggressively managed pooled funds that operate in all markets, from stocks to derivatives.

UNIT TRUSTS

Are unincorporated pooled funds, formed under a trust deed. They have an unlimited number of shares, so their managers may issue or cancel units, whichever is necessary. Unit trusts invest in securities but don't reinvest the returns from investment; instead, they reward their individual unit holders.

INVESTMENT TRUSTS

Are publicly listed pool funds that issue a fixed number of shares that are quoted on a stock market. The share price of an investment trust is influenced by the market, i.e., demand and supply.

REITS

Real Estate Investment Trusts are firms that pool funds to invest in properties in the real estate market. They own and manage both commercial and residential properties. If you want a low-risk investment that is completely inflation-proof, or you are interested in real estate but do not want to buy the actual property to avoid the management hassle that accompanies it, REITs are a great option for you.

ETFS

An Exchange Traded Fund tracks a basket of securities and trades like stock on the share market. You can learn more about these in my starter guide to stocks.

INDEX FUNDS

These funds follow the performance of a particular market index; therefore its securities are automatically picked. Besides the low operating costs, it covers virtually all industries and provides low portfolio turnover.

OTHER TYPES OF INVESTMENTS

REAL ESTATE

Real estate investors buy property as a form of investment. This includes commercial and residential buildings as well as idle land. Returns are made in terms of property appreciation, rent and lease income.

FOREX

Investing in the FOREX (Foreign Exchange) market involves the purchasing of currencies that the investor has a bias on the appreciation of. It essentially involves buying undervalued currencies in the hope of selling them at a higher price in future.

PRECIOUS METALS AND COMMODITIES

The concept used in investing in precious metals and commodities is similar to that of FOREX investments. It involves buying precious metals and commodities at a low price with the hope of selling them at a higher price in future. Precious metals include gold and silver, while commodities include soya beans, wheat, and corn. Oil is also classified as a commodity.

As a beginner, it is understandable that you may be overwhelmed by the wide array of investment opportunities available. Place that concern aside for now, because in the coming chapters we will discover how to align yourself to a particular investment choice using three key factors: risk tolerance, time and investment goals.

Once you understand how to do that, you will be able to come back and see exactly which investment opportunities are right for you.

CHAPTER SUMMARY

- Investors have many different options to choose from.
- Your choice will depend on your goals for investing, risk tolerance and time constraints (covered next).

CREATING A WINNING INVESTING PLAN

❧

Investing is a journey, and one has to prepare for it. As a beginner, you don't want to throw your hard earned cash at anything without a clear plan.

An investor has to identify his or her reasons for investing and the goals he or she wants to achieve. The development of an investment plan to achieve these goals is the next step.

An investment plan should include clearly defined investment goals. You will need to ask yourself the following questions and think hard on the answers.

- "Why do I want to invest?"
- "What goals do I want to achieve?"
- "How much disposable income do I have?"
- "How long do I have to achieve my goals?"

These are crucial questions for every investor to answer, from rookies to the richest men and women in the world.

WHY

Starting by asking yourself why you wish to invest. This is not the same as setting goals, where you will get specific, but rather your 'big picture'. Do you want to earn a little extra disposable income, or perhaps build a vast portfolio to take care of your family for generations to come?

Different people have different priorities, often depending on their stage of life. A youthful investor may want to buy his or her first car, while a young family may prioritize buying a new home. On the other hand a retiree may simply be concerned about increasing his income and focusing more on financial security.

I encourage you to take out a pen and paper right now and brainstorm your biggest 'whys' about investing. You will carry these with you throughout your investment journey.

HOW

Your goals are the 'how' to your 'why', and may include the amount of return desired, and what you will do with those returns to bring you closer to your target. By considering your financial plans for the future, investments can be well directed to and subsequently keep you right on track.

Once you have set your sights on a target, it's time to assess your current financial status and then set out a time-specific plan.

CURRENT FINANCIAL POSITION

Investing requires capital. For this reason, a potential investor should analyze his or her current financial standing so as to determine how much disposable income or wealth is available for investment purposes.

Some of the things to look at in this step include:

TOTAL ASSETS

This is the process of accounting for all of the money and commodities you have to your name. Though the figure may not be accurate to the penny, it should give a good enough idea of the current financial health of the potential investor.

In accounting terms, this includes looking at current assets, which include money in the bank and savings, and some fixed assets such as your home and car.

It is good practice not to include money still held by debtors since there is a chance of defaulting on repayment.

CURRENT DEBT STATUS

This step is mostly overlooked by potential and beginner investors. However, finding out how much is owed to other people is a very important part of investing.

Performing this step helps keep the investor stable and also protects the investments from the creditors (liability protection).

Common debts that people have include mortgages, car loans, credit card balances, student finance and other outstanding bills.

NET WORTH

This is the figure calculated based on the previous two steps: total financial assets minus debt.

Many wake up to the rude realization that they have a negative net worth at this stage. Those that unfortunately find themselves in this situation should review their expenditures and try to increase their income before investing. They may also explore alternative ways to fund their investments, for instance, bank loans or venture capital. These options are beyond the scope of this guide as they are generally not viable options for beginners.

CHAPTER SUMMARY

As we have seen, the investment options available for both beginners and professional investors can be overwhelming. To select the right investment, every beginner investor should make a personalized list of what he or she wants to accomplish through investing within a specified timeframe, and budget accordingly.

In this chapter, we have looked at the preliminary steps that a potential or beginner investor should take. This includes goal setting and analyzing their current financial net worth.

Here is a summary of some of the questions serious beginner or potential investors should ask themselves before making their first move:

- Why do I want to invest?
- What are my goals that will enable me to achieve my desired outcomes?
- How long am I willing to wait to achieve these investment goals?
- How much money is available for investing?
- These questions pay off in a big way in the long run. For those that want to bypass this part, they may consider consulting financial planners to do the work for them.
- Remember, nobody else can tell you your 'why,' even if they can do the rest of the legwork.

UNDERSTANDING & MITIGATING RISK

As an investor purchasing an asset, you are faced with two unknowns; you may not know the future price at which you can sell the asset, and you may not know the amount you'll receive in payment for ownership of the asset. The degree of this variability or uncertainty of return on an asset, or the inability to predict the future value of this asset, is what is described as the investment risk.

For example, if you buy 100 shares of Facebook Inc., today at $114, you cannot know its future price, because just like any stock, its share price changes continually. While you can be sure that you will earn dividends, you cannot ascertain exactly how much you will receive as it is not a commitment, but rather a discretionary payment whose figure is subject to change.

While bonds and treasury bills are investments, this type of risk may not directly apply to them given that the maturity value and payment of bonds are set out at the onset of investment. However, the price of bonds fluctuate, and there is a risk of default should they be redeemed prematurely. Another underlying factor is that the real value of a bond is uncertain as the maturity value of any bond is given in nominal terms and may not take into account the effect of inflation.

RELATIONSHIP BETWEEN RISK AND RETURN

Every investor must factor the reward of holding an asset and the risk that comes with it. As a potential investor, you must also know the relationship between risk and returns, particularly when your investments are combined to form a portfolio.

The ultimate truth in investment is that the market rewards those who are willing to bear the risk. It is generally accepted that the higher the risk, the higher the rewards because the return on investment is directly proportional to the risk inherent in holding that investment.

Below is a risk curve explaining the risk levels of different assets in relation to their respective returns.

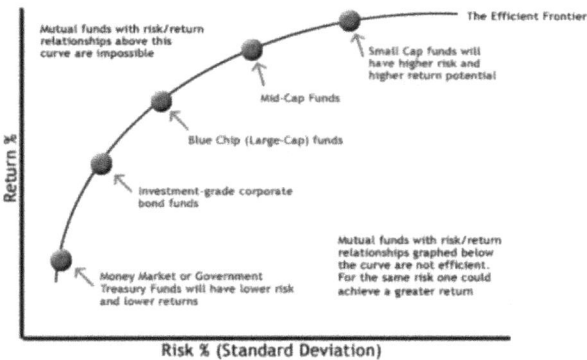

FACTORS THAT INFLUENCE RISK

We can classify risk using several variables that constitute the risk of making any particular investment. To better understand these classes, let us first look at the factors.

The risk level of an investment is influenced by:

TIMEFRAME

The longer the timeframe of an investment, the riskier it is. Over time, a lot of things can change. For instance, the maturity value of the investment may be eroded by inflation, or if it is denominated in a foreign currency, it could be eroded by fluctuation in exchange rates. In the case of bonds, a longer timeline increases the chances of the issuer defaulting on payment.

LIQUIDITY

How quickly can you turn your investment into cash? If you can't sell your asset the moment you need your money, then you are likely to sell it at a throwaway price. An investment that lacks liquidity is highly risky.

UNDERLYING ACTIVITIES

In the stock market, a firm's activities determine the risk of investing in its stock. In essence, firms that operate in established industries such as energy are less risky than those in relatively new or dynamic fields like ICT.

CREDITWORTHINESS OF THE ISSUER

In the bond market, there are countries or corporations with low credit ratings resulting from poor credit history. Bonds from such issuers, though lucrative, are highly risky.

PRIORITY

There are two classes of stocks, preferential and common. In a firm, common stockholders fall last in the priority line after bondholders and other creditors. Should a firm default on payment, bondholders can put it into bankruptcy. Preferential shareholders have priority over their counterparts in laying claims on the firm's assets, but they merely get the residual after the bondholders and other creditors have claimed their fair share.

CLASSES OF RISK

From the factors outlined above, we can classify investments into different risk classes, which include:

LIQUIDITY RISK

This would happen if you are interested in selling an investment you hold but there is no buyer in the market to facilitate the trade. The investment then becomes void, as you, the investor, would be stuck with an investment you can't cash in.

NATIONAL RISK

Investments are tied to their respective native countries or geographical regions. Hence, factors affecting the welfare of such countries or geographic regions are also likely to affect the investments made in those areas.

Natural disasters and financial constraints in particular areas affect investments made in those places adversely. One major factor that has been affecting investments in some countries is political unrest. Countries that have been experiencing political upheavals make the environment very unfavorable for investments to thrive.

MARKET RISK

This is more relevant in financial markets such as stocks. The returns in these financial asset classes tend to fluctuate from time to time, making it difficult to pinpoint when the returns are going to be favorable.

CURRENCY RISK

Most world currencies use a floating exchange rate regime. It follows that the values of the currencies are susceptible to changing market conditions and hence fluctuate occasionally. This brings rise to a considerable rate of risk since an investor cannot pinpoint exactly what is going to happen to the exchange rate in the future.

INFLATION RISK

In times of inflation, the value of goods and services tend to soar, weakening purchasing power and consequently reducing the value of returns expected by investors.

VOLATILITY RISK

It was earlier mentioned that investments are mainly made to achieve long-term financial goals. This is because most investments experience periods of high volatility. Volatility simply means the deviation of returns from the expected mean.

Though the overall performance of the investment may be as expected; it is met from time to time with periods of volatility and, for this reason, most investors tend to focus on the long-term return on their investment.

CONCENTRATION RISK

This type of risk arises when asset allocation and investment diversification are not executed properly, such that a large chunk of an investor's money is put in one type of investment.

If you concentrate your investments in a particular industry, and that industry experiences an economic downturn, you could lose all of your investment or suffer massive losses. For instance, investors who concentrated their investment in the banking sector before the 2008 global financial crisis suffered huge losses.

CREDIT RISK

This type of risk will occur mostly with investments backed by a particular body or organization. If the backing body collapses or becomes bankrupt, then the investment also liquidates.

CHAPTER SUMMARY

- The higher the potential return on investment, the greater the risk attached.
- Conservative investors only willing to make very low-risk investments must accept low rates of return, and vice versa.

DIVERSIFICATION & ASSET ALLOCATION

We now know that investing involves a considerable risk of loss. This chapter aims to equip you with two risk management strategies; asset allocation and diversification.

ASSET ALLOCATION

This refers to balancing the amounts available for investment between different investment classes that make up your portfolio.

As we have already established, there are a host of investment options available, all of which have different characteristics as summarized in the table below. Asset allocation involves investing in unrelated investment instruments in a bid to accomplish your investment goals.

ROBERT EATON

Asset class	Key characteristics	Potentially suitable for
Equities	Potential for capital growth, and may offer income through the payment of dividends. You can choose to invest in UK and overseas companies.	Medium-to-long-term investors (five years plus).
Bonds	Can provide a steady and reliable income stream with potential for capital growth and usually offers a higher interest rate, or yield, than cash. Includes UK government bonds (gilts), overseas government bonds, and company loans (corporate bonds).	Short, medium or long-term investors.
Property	Provides the benefits of diversification through access to properties in retail, office, industrial, tourism and infrastructure sectors. You can invest in both UK and international property.	Medium-to-long-term investors (five years plus).
Cash	May be suitable for short-term needs, such as an impending down payment on a new home. Usually includes higher interest paying securities, as well as bank and building society accounts or term deposits (a cash deposit at a financial institution that has a fixed term).	Short-term investors (up to three years).

The task of dividing the investment amount between different asset classes, for instance, stocks, bonds and real estate, is an individual investor's decision.

Asset allocation is mainly governed by the investor's risk tolerance. An investor with a high-risk tolerance will put more investment funds in riskier assets.

Asset allocation is mainly based on the following factors:

INVESTMENT TIME HORIZON

This is the time period within which the investor expects his or her investment to have achieved its set goals. As discussed in the risk section of this guide, long-term investors can cope with volatility risk since they are focused on long-term returns. Such investors will choose riskier securities, as they are not concerned with the short-term volatility cycle that may cause short-term investors to panic.

INVESTOR'S RISK TOLERANCE LEVEL

As you will hear over and over, higher returns inherently carry greater risks. An investor who has a high level of risk tolerance will invest more in highly risky assets and hence gain greater returns. Conservative investors, on the other hand, will often invest in low-risk asset classes to get moderate returns.

DIVERSIFICATION

In investment, diversification is the method of spreading investment choices among a variety of securities, industries, and any other category.

We have all heard the famous saying, 'don't put all your eggs in one basket.' The reasoning behind this saying is very clear. In investing, it can be translated to 'do not put all your investment funds in one type of investment'.

You spread the choice of assets in your portfolio to reduce the risk involved in case one type of investment experiences poor returns. There are two levels of diversification: between investment types and within a particular investment type.

Diversification between investment types involves investing in unrelated investments, for instance, stocks, real estate and fixed income securities.

Conversely, diversification within an asset class encompasses investing in differently behaving instruments in that class. In the case of stocks, this could be spreading your investment to include large cap/blue chip stocks, growth stocks, and value stocks.

We can, therefore, define diversification as a risk management strategy that prevents the investor from investing much or all of their funds in one particular type of investment. In contrast, asset allocation deals with balancing the total investment amount between different classes of investments in a way that ensures maximum return depending on the investor's investment goals.

CHAPTER SUMMARY

- Risk cannot be eliminated, but it can be managed to suitable levels.
- Asset allocation is targeted at driving more returns on investment. Having the right mix of investment types may

increase returns significantly.

- Diversification minimizes chances of suffering a total loss in investment.

CALCULATING RETURNS ON INVESTMENTS

Return can be defined as the change in the value of an asset over a specified period as a proportion of an asset's initial value. Essentially, return is the rate at which an investment makes profit or loss.

$$\text{Return} = \frac{(V1 - V0)}{V0}$$

Where:

V0 = the initial value of the asset

V1 = the new value of the asset

RETURNS ON STOCKS

Returns must capture the rate at which a security is increasing the investor's wealth. So, when calculating return on stocks, one must include dividends (capital gains).

Dividends are paid twice a year in the U.K. and in each quarter in the U.S. To calculate the return on investing in a specified stock in one year, the dividends for the whole year must be factored in.

$$\text{Return on Stock} = \frac{(P1 + d) - P0}{P0}$$

Where;

P0 = buying price of the stock

P1 = its trading price

d = total dividend collected over the period

Example:

Walter invested in Facebook Inc, (NASDAQ: FB), in Jan 2014 buying 1000 shares of the stock at $80.96 each. For the four quarters of 2014, the social media giant rewarded its shareholders with dividend payments of $0.15, $0.15, $0.15 and $0.16. The stock closed trading in 2014 trading at $87.57.

The returns on Walter's investment in 2014 can be calculated as follows:

$$r = \frac{\$(87.57 \times 100 + 0.61 \times 100) - (\$80.96 \times 100)}{(80.96 \times 100)}$$

=0.089

Where:

P0 = $80.96

P1 = $87.57

d = $0.61

The actual monetary value of Walter's investment can be calculated as follows:

Total dividend = $0.61 x 1000 = $610

New share price = $87.57

Value of investment based on share price = $87570

Actual value of investment =$87570 + $610

= $88180

Alternatively, you can arrive at this figure by using the percentage return:

Initial investment = $80960

Return = 8.917%

$88179.44

NB: The slight difference in the figure is brought about by the approximation of percentage rate.

BONDS AND RETURN

As discussed earlier, a bond is a debt instrument used by governments and corporations to raise funds. These corporations/governments are the issuers, while the investor is the bondholder. The bondholder is entitled to a periodic interest payment until the bond matures.

When dealing with bonds, return on the invested capital is called the yield. Other aspects of yield that you will come across in the bond market include:

COUPON YIELD (COUPON RATE)

This is the established annual interest rate that the bond pays. It is expressed as a percentage of the bond's par value, and it remains unchanged until the maturity of the bond.

Example:

A bond bought for $1,000 that receives $65 p.a. in interest payments will have a coupon yield of 6.5%. Here is how we arrive at that figure:

$$\text{coupon yield} = \frac{\$65}{\$1000} \times 100\%$$

= 6.5%

CURRENT YIELD:

This is the bond's coupon rate expressed as a fraction of its market price. Current yield, as the name would suggest, works with the current price of a bond and is used to determine the return if held until maturity (one year).

Example:

If the bond in the above example is trading at 105 ($1050), then the current yield will be as follows:

$$\text{current yield} = \frac{6.5}{105} \times 100$$

= 6.19%

And if it later trades at 103 ($1030), then the current yield would be:

$$\text{current yield} = \frac{6.5}{103} \times 100$$

= 6.31%

If the bond is bought at par and held to maturity then:

$$\text{Coupon yield} = \text{Current Yield}$$

YIELD TO MATURITY (YTM)

If an investor buys a bond at the prevailing market price and holds it to the specified redemption date, the overall interest earned is referred to as 'yield to maturity'. YTM is arrived at by adding the discounted bond coupons and principal payment and expressing the total as a fraction of the bond's market price. Its calculation ignores taxes and any brokerage costs incurred.

YIELD TO CALL (YTC)

A bond investor may redeem his investment before the maturity date. This date is known as the call date. The total interest earned until the bond is redeemed is referred to as the 'yield to call'. Its calculation is more or less the same as the YTM, save for the fact that YTC is based on the call date and not maturity.

YIELD TO WORST (YTW)

After calculating a bond's YTM and YTC, whichever is lower is the YTW.

In the bond market, when the price of a bond increases, its yield decreases, and the reverse is also true. In simple terms, the price and yield are inversely related.

It is important to note that the calculation of YTM and YTC are based on three assumptions and are therefore only estimates. These three assumptions are that:

- Bondholders hold their investment to maturity or call date.
- Every coupon is reinvested at the same rate. However, the interest rate on a bond is determined by the market forces, hence it fluctuates. Consequently, the interest on the reinvestment varies.
- Coupons are reinvested at the YTM or YTC.

How to calculate return on bonds:

The formula for calculating return on bonds will be familiar by now:

$$r = \frac{(V1 + d) - V0}{V0}$$

Where:

r = returns on a bond

V0 = the initial value of the principle (the amount invested in the bond)

V1 = the new value of the principle

d = the difference between the sum of coupon and compound interests, and the sum of commissions/fees and taxes

Therefore, return on bonds is calculated as follows:

$$r = \frac{[\{End\ Value\ of\ Principal\ +\ Coupon\ Interest\ +\ Compound\ Interest\} - \{Taxes\ +\ Fees\}] - Initial\ Value\ of\ Principle}{Initial\ Value\ of\ Principal}$$

NB: Compound interest is explained later in this chapter.

RETURN AND MATURITY OF A BOND

The return on a bond goes up as the holding period increases, as explained by the following yield curve.

Yield

Upward Sloping Treasury Yield Curve

6

5

4

3

2

1

0

1 month   1 year   2 years   3 years   5 years   7 years   10 years   20 years

Maturity

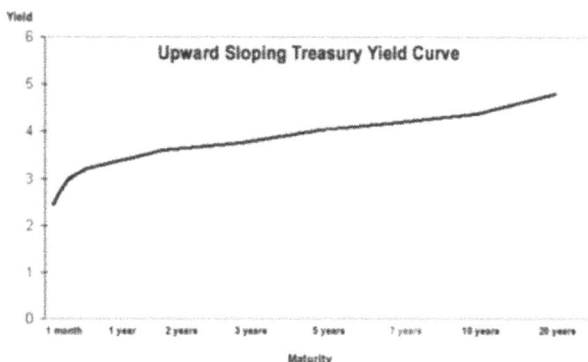

From the above curve, a 30-day T-bill will earn about 2.5% p.a. while a 20-year bond will earn about 4.8% p.a.

While interpreting a yield curve, a relatively flat upward-slope implies an extremely minimal difference between returns from a short-term bond and a long-term one.

As we have covered, the risk attached to holding a bond increases as the holding period increases, so it is prudent for an investor to weigh the risk of buying a 10 or 20-year bond for moderately higher interest against holding a short-term bond with a modest interest rate.

There is more to learn about bonds, but as a beginner the above will serve you well.

RETURNS ON A PORTFOLIO

A portfolio is an array of securities such as bonds, stocks, or cash equivalents held by an investor or organization.

We have already discovered how to calculate returns on an individual asset, but how do you calculate the returns on a portfolio held by an investor?

The method we've used in calculating returns on an individual asset is still applicable to the calculation of returns on a portfolio. However, you must note the difference in what the variables represent.

$$r = \frac{(V1 + d) - V0}{V0}$$

Where:

r = returns on a portfolio

V0 = the sum of the initial values of the assets that make up the portfolio

V1 = the sum of the new values of the assets that make up the portfolio

d = the sum of interests and dividends earned by the individual assets in the portfolio

These formulas should be looking familiar by now, so you will find that simple variations are incredibly easy to factor in when making your calculations.

COMPOUND INTEREST

The return on investment is the primary reason why an investor may choose to hold the investment. The duration the investment is held, referred to as the 'holding period', plays a crucial role in determining the return of the investment, and there is no better way to explain it than the old adage, 'time is money'.

Through the principle of compounding, long-term investors can magnify their returns on investment, particularly if the interest on the principle amount is reinvested.

Albert Einstein regarded compounding as "the greatest mathematical discovery of all time". Understanding the principle of compounding will make a huge difference in one's investments and life at large. It can bring about new levels of financial freedom for an investor.

The concept has been applied in various areas and sectors, but its best application is in investing. The basics involve reinvesting earnings gotten previously so as to accelerate the growth of an investment. By doing this, one earns interest on the initial sum of capital invested as well as the prior interest. For clarity, let's look at a simple demonstration.

Example:

Let's say you invest 100 dollars in the stock market, generating an average return of 20% annually. In the first year, your earnings would be:

$100 X 0.2 = $20

To compound your earnings, the second year you would invest the total amount of $120, hence in the second year, your returns would be:

$120 X 0.2 = $24 giving a total of $144 which would be reinvested for the third year.

The formula for calculating compound interest is:

$$r = \frac{(V1 + d) - V0}{V0}$$

Where:

P = the principal (the initial investment amount)

r = the rate of return (in our previous example, 0.2)

n = number of interest/return periods per year

t = number of years the investment has been active

A = this will be the total return after the investment period

Given the formula, and using our earlier example, let's calculate how much money one would generate investing just $100 within a period of 20 years.

P = $100, r = 0.2, n = 1, and t = 20

A = $100 (1 + 0.2/1) ^1(20)

A = $3, 833.76

Compounding one hundred dollars at 0.2 rate of interest over 20 years would have made 38 times more than the initial investment.

New investors should set aside a particular amount of their disposable income for investment as early as possible so as to capitalize on the concept of compounding early. This is because the initial investment does not only determine earnings got from compounding, but also the amount of time one has to keep reinvesting the earned interest plus principal.

This should then be coupled with the rate of return that the investment offers. An investment that offers high levels of return will utilize the compounding principle far better and amass a lot of wealth for the investor.

CHAPTER SUMMARY

- The motivation behind investing is the reward, or return on capital invested.
- Return is the profit or capital gain an investor gets for risking his capital.
- For compound interest to take place, restitution on investment or interest must be added to the initial investment amount (principal).

- The more time someone has to reinvest his or her earnings, the more earnings they will receive due to compounding.
- Albert Einstein also described compounding as "the most powerful force of the universe."
- Anybody who can afford to put away any amount of money can benefit from compound interest by reinvesting interest earned on the initial investment.
- Another underlying principle of compound interest is the sacrifice of today's spending by saving or investing so as to reap huge rewards in future.

SMART INVESTMENT SELECTION

This section will help you to identify investment assets to form your portfolio and realize your investment objectives. Consider this chapter as a means of putting everything you have learnt so far into a powerful personal strategy.

We have already covered in depth the fundamental aspects of making an investment; risk vs returns. Now it's time to begin constructing your investment portfolio.

PORTFOLIO CONSTRUCTION ROADMAP

Portfolio construction begins with identifying your investment objectives, which we addressed in chapter 3, and takes into account everything you've already learnt. Here are the basic steps:

1. IDENTIFY INVESTMENT OBJECTIVES

As discussed, you must have an investment policy that guides your investment decisions. This is of cardinal importance as far as your investment selection and portfolio construction are concerned. The policy includes your reasons for investing, and your targets and timeframe for achieving the set objectives.

2. DETERMINE DISPOSABLE INCOME

The second decision concerns the amount you have available to spend. You must have set aside a specific amount you want to use to realize your set goals. There are many classes of securities, and you should decide the amount you want to invest now and the amount you want to hold on to for future investment opportunities.

3. CHOOSE CLASSES OF INVESTMENTS

This should be based on your investment goals and objectives. As a beginner, it would be advisable for you to avoid complicated investment instruments such as derivatives. The best options for a beginner are generally thought to be basic securities such as bonds and stocks.

4. ANALYZE INVESTMENT OPTIONS

While the bulk of investment analysis is usually handled by specialists, there are a few things that an informed beginner can determine. You must conduct a study of any potential investment option, paying particular attention to its prospective returns and accompanying risk. This study will help you to determine which assets to buy in a specified investment class. For example, it may help you to avoid falling prey to overpriced assets while taking advantage of the underpriced ones.

There are two ways of analyzing an investment:

- Technical Analysis: This is the study of historical price patterns and trends to establish future price trends. It helps an investor predict the best time to buy or sell an asset. However, this approach may be overly complicated for a beginner.
- Fundamental Analysis: The act of studying the performance of a company by concentrating on its activities to predict profitability. Fundamental analysis focuses on the real value of an investment based on its future returns.

There is lots of expert analytical information freely available online, so you can easily obtain data on a stock you want to invest in and compare it with others before making a decision.

5. PORTFOLIO CONSTRUCTION

After analysis, you can make an informed decision as to which assets you wish to place your hard earned cash into. It is here that you apply the asset allocation and diversification strategies covered in chapter five. You must decide how much to spend on each of the chosen investment instruments.

Factors to consider when putting together a portfolio include the spread of risk, transaction costs and the difficulty level of managing the investment products. Portfolio construction is a complex business, which is why most investors seek an expert opinion at this stage.

6. INVESTMENT EVALUATION

At this stage, you will assess the performance of your chosen investment or portfolio. The best way to do this is by comparing returns on investment with another investment with similar risk properties.

CHAPTER SUMMARY

- In this section we have covered the criteria and strategies used to select investments.
- There are six stages in choosing an investment.
- Objectives and the amount available for investment are key factors in deciding what investment product to choose.
- Fundamental and technical analyses are used to predict assets with favorable prospects.

MANAGING YOUR INVESTMENT PORTFOLIO

You have found the right combination of securities according to your objectives, and through asset allocation and diversification you have selected your securities. Now it is time to monitor the investments and see how they perform.

You need to review your investment products periodically. While reviewing your investment portfolio, you should start with your objectives and work down through the entire process of investment selection. You need to align the investment products to your investment objectives, which may have changed over time.

You can manage your assets by yourself or employ professional management services through pooled funds.

DIY

If you are a 'do-it-yourself' type, there are three core issues you must address while managing your assets:

ASSET ALLOCATION

You have already populated your portfolio with actual investments. However, while reviewing them, you need to ensure the asset allocation of these products is in line with your strategy. If they are not aligned, it is it time to reallocate.

DIVERSIFICATION

Whereas diversification will not assure you of profits, it helps you mitigate the risk of losing your money. It will also help you to dilute the impact of a volatile market. So be sure that your portfolio or investment products meet the diversification requirement.

PERFORMANCE

Performance of a specified asset may have changed, or there could be better investment options available than the one you have in your portfolio. You can drop the nonperforming asset and substitute it with a new one, but be careful; you don't want to make a rash decision that you might regret.

USING POOLED FUNDS

Pooled funds are professional investment management companies that combine investors' monies in a fund and invest them in a range of investment products. For examples of pooled funds, see mutual funds in chapter two.

These funds, therefore, give an investor the opportunity to invest in a diversified portfolio without much stress.

An investor's share is proportionate to his/her investment in the fund, and he/she enjoys returns and other income based on that share.

A fund is professionally managed and the investment decisions made are well informed. It may invest in stocks, debt instruments, real estate, or a combination of these assets as long as it is in line with its objective.

The funds can either be actively or passively managed.

ACTIVE MANAGEMENT

An actively managed fund consists of professionals who pick stocks.

The aim of the fund is to beat its index. For clarity, an index is a collection of assets (e.g. stocks, bonds or properties) representing a segment of the market.

To achieve the fund's goal, the managers use either a top-down or bottom-up approach:

- Top-Down: The managers begin by studying the economic trends to predict the sectors of the economy with a bright future. They then identify the most promising stocks.
- Bottom-Up: The managers choose the best securities in any industry and assume that the stock will perform regardless of the situation in the industry.

Active managers research and make judgment calls on which assets to sell and which to hold.

PASSIVE MANAGEMENT

Passively managed funds follow a particular index and therefore do not require the managers to handpick stocks.

For example, the Standard & Poor's 500, abbreviated as the S&P 500, is a renowned index that tracks 500 large companies listed on the American stock markets (NYSE or NASDAQ).

The size of each company in the index is based on the market value of its outstanding shares, known as its market capitalization. A fund that tracks such an index does not require the manager to pick the stocks, for the pick is automatic.

Such a fund will buy shares of every company tracked by the index, so the fund's performance will reflect that of the index.

ADVANTAGES OF POOLED FUNDS

Pooled funds are a great solution for anyone lacking the time or complete knowledge to make 100% of their investment decisions. Let's find out why.

PROFESSIONAL MANAGEMENT

The funds have professional managers and researchers to screen out the best investments according to their firm's objective.

COST EFFICIENCY

By letting an investment fund invest for you, you may get more out of your investment capital than if you decide to do it yourself.

DIVERSIFICATION

These funds, particularly index funds, invest in an array of products; therefore you can spread risk across the market.

LIQUIDITY

You can quickly turn your investment in these funds into cash. Exchange traded funds and investment trusts are the most liquid as they trade publicly like shares.

DISADVANTAGES OF POOLED FUNDS

As with any form of investing, there are pitfalls to pooled funds too. Let's look at those now.

COSTS

Professional management comes at a cost. These funds impose charges to cater for their day-to-day operations. Additionally, when you trade the funds, they charge commission. These different costs will impact your return on investment.

GOALS

The fund may not accurately meet your investment objective. If the fund is not aligned with your own objectives, your investment may not run smoothly.

DIVERSIFICATION

This may limit you from the capital gains associated with an individual security that may not have been covered by the fund.

NO GUARANTEES

There is no guarantee that the investor will get back more than he or she invested. As a matter of fact, the price of traded funds fluctuates the same way shares do. The incomes from these funds also vary, and investors may even make a loss. This, of course, is true of all investment options.

CHAPTER SUMMARY

- It is important to regularly evaluate the performance of your portfolio or investments.
- Your assets must at all times be in line with your investment goals; they must be performing well and be sufficiently diverse.
- You can choose to use pooled funds to avoid the stress of managing your investments.
- Pooled funds are either actively or passively managed.
- The stocks monitored by actively managed funds are handpicked by managers, while those of their passively managed counterparts are automatic.
- Using funds has both its merits and drawbacks.

BENEFITS OF INVESTING

We have already shown how you can achieve long-term financial goals via investing. We broke down goals such as purchasing a home, paying for college or securing retirement and put together a plan of action. Now let's dive deeper into the benefits that you as a potential or beginner investor stand to enjoy.

LONG-TERM EARNINGS OR RETURNS

Through investing, one is likely to increase his or her wealth by significant amounts in the long run. Though this also carries an inherent risk of loss, it is one of the most efficient ways to amass great wealth.

REDUCE THE EFFECT OF INFLATION

Through making investments, one can earn a rate of return or interest that exceeds the rate of inflation. The net return on investments after any tax deductible should be greater than the rate of inflation.

For this reason, most people choose investments over savings since savings offer a much lower rate of return compared to investments.

Beginner investors should look for the investment opportunities that will give a rate of return that beats inflation.

INCOME GENERATION

You can make investments so as to provide for your regular income needs. This would require investments that have much lesser periods of maturity as well as regular intervals of return.

With such investments, an investor would be assured of stable revenues now and then. Those investing for the sake of their retirement also enjoy the income benefit of investing; after their retirement, they continue to earn income from their investments.

BENEFITS OF INVESTING EARLY

There are some aspects of investing that lend themselves particularly well to younger people. Let's explore some of those now.

TIME

Younger investors have more years of investing ahead of them than the older population. Most importantly, they have much more time to learn the ropes.

They also have more opportunities to learn from their successes and repeat the processes over and over, hence accruing much more wealth. Simply put, young investors have time to take on the investment learning curve.

Young people, and by way, that is really anybody who isn't well into retirement already, are also in a position to indulge in more risky investments since they have ample time to recover. Someone already investing for retirement, on the other hand, does not have the time advantage of taking great risks in investments that offer high returns since they also pose a bigger risk of loss.

COMPOUNDING

As covered previously, the ingredients of compounding include initial capital as well as time. Investing early means you will have many years of reinvesting interest earned ahead of you, equating to much greater returns.

IMPROVED QUALITY OF LIFE

Investing at a young age provides an opportunity to get ahead of the pack and hence achieve most of your financial goals early on in life, leaving you financially free to pursue your passions.

MORE INVESTMENT OPPORTUNITIES

Early investors have more investment opportunities to choose from. For instance, someone who started investing four decades ago had a chance to invest in some of the investment opportunities that offered a higher return then, but are now overcrowded.

Chapter Summary:

- Investing can work for anyone, it is simply a matter of establishing your goals and planning to meet them.
- The earlier you invest, the greater your opportunities.
- It is never too late to put your money to work!

TIPS FROM THE GREATS

As mentioned in the previous chapter, investing involves a learning curve. Some people emerge as better investors than others. However, there are those that have stood the test of time and raked in stunning returns over the course of their careers.

These esteemed investors have amassed great wealth for themselves as well as those who invested in their funds. Each of these investors has utilized their own unique strategy of making investments that stood out and provided positive returns year after year. Let's take a look at them now.

BENJAMIN GRAHAM

Benjamin Graham was born in London in 1894 and died in 1976. He was both a financial educator as well as an investment manager. Investment stakeholders often regard Graham as "the father of value investing".

One of his published books, 'The Intelligent Investor' (1949), contains a lot of investing principles and philosophies still referenced by modern day investors and educational institutions. He also taught and mentored other top investors including Warren Buffet.

It is important to point out that Graham suffered a massive loss in the 1929 stock market crash. However, like most professional investors, he learnt from his mistakes and went on to write another excellent book, 'Security Analysis', which also became a financial classic.

Benjamin Graham was affiliated with the investment firm Graham-Newman in partnership with another great investor, Jerome Newman. His primary investment principle was that investments should be undervalued at the time the investor invests.

WARREN BUFFET

Another great investor, Warren Buffet, was born in Nebraska in 1930. Most people view Buffet as one of the greatest investors in history. Through his firm, Berkshire Hathaway, Buffet followed Benjamin Graham's investment principles and amassed billions of dollars for himself as well as his fund.

Warren Buffet studied Graham's book, 'The Intelligent Investor', and later studied under the man himself at Columbia University. He went on to land a job at Graham's company, Graham-Newman and worked side-by-side with Benjamin Graham. This relationship with Graham created the foundation for Buffet's investing principles.

Today, he remains affiliated with Berkshire Hathaway. One of Warren Buffet's greatest quotes is: "Rule number one is never lose money. Rule number two is never forget rule number one."

JESSE L. LIVERMORE

Jesse L. Livermore was born in Massachusetts in 1877 and died in 1940. He was not affiliated with any fund and acted as an individual investor. During his investment career in the stock market, Jesse Livermore made huge losses as well as massive profits.

He was an investor as early as the age of fifteen. With no formal education at all, his trading skills were horned directly by participating in the market.

Unfortunately, Jesse Livermore died in 1940 through suicide. One famous quote by Jesse Livermore is "profits always take care of themselves, but losses never do."

GEORGE SOROS

George Soros was born in Budapest in 1930. He is mainly affiliated with the Quantum Fund. George Soros is most famous for risking ten billion dollars against the British Pound in 1992. On that single day, he made approximately a billion dollars in return.

Soros was particularly good in bonds and currencies, making short-term speculations. One of his greatest publications is 'The Alchemy of Finance' (1988). Today, George Soros is one of the world's biggest philanthropists, donating large sums of his wealth worldwide.

One of Soros' greatest quotes is, "It's not whether you're right or wrong that's important, but how much money you make when you are right and how much money you lose when you are wrong."

CHAPTER SUMMARY

• If you want to be the best, learn from the best and discover more about these greats.

QUICK START GUIDE

"An investment in knowledge pays interest!" - Benjamin Franklin.

Anyone can become a successful investor; all it takes is commitment, focus, and discipline paired with honesty, and patience. By picking up this book, you have already made a bold step in becoming not just another investor, but a smart one. Consider it as an investment that will pay you back in kind.

Before you picked up this book, you had a dream about your future. What you've learnt in it will guide you towards achieving that dream.

You've discovered that before you start the investment process, you must first know three things about yourself; your goals, time limit, and risk tolerance. So use these to develop your investment plan and, together with everything else you've learnt in this guide, begin your journey to financial independence. Always remember to keep an open eye at costs.

WHERE NEXT?

There are a variety of investment options open to you; it is the depth of your pockets that will decide which to choose. If you want to start small, meaning with as little as $20, perhaps the best option for you would be a Direct Stock Purchase Plan (DSPP) and its peer Dividend Reinvestment Plan (DRIP). Through these options, you don't have to buy a full share, but you'll need to setup an automatic investment plan that will enable you to invest small amounts at a predetermined frequency.

Alternatively, if you have relatively modest savings for investment, let's say $500, then maybe the right option for you would be index funds. Why index funds? The initial investment required by these funds may be as little as $250, and you get at least 10% returns annually on your invested capital. What's more, once you make the initial investment, the subsequent investments have no conditions, fees or commissions attached.

If you don't fit into either of the two groups covered above, or if you have $1000 or more to invest, then your investment horizon is much broader. Consider opening an account with a brokerage service provider and invest in stocks. Here, though, you need to be a little more vigilant regarding fees and commissions charged by brokerage firms. Some charge exorbitantly high fees but don't reciprocate it in the quality of services they offer.

So, the amount you have available for the purpose of investing should not be an obstacle to getting started. You don't have to shy away from investing because you think the money you have is not sufficient. If you want to accumulate wealth, you have to make investing a habit. There are no excuses now; you have laid a strong foundation and can get started with as little as $20.

Your dreams are castles in the air and, as Henry David Thoreau put it, "If you have built castles in the air, your work need not be lost; that is where they should be. Now put the foundations under them."

So go ahead, continue your learning in practice, and take positive strides towards achieving your wildest dreams through financial independence. It's all possible thanks to the magic of investing.

CONCLUSION

As a potential or beginner investor at any stage in life, it is wise to pick up good investment habits to secure your future.

Financial freedom can be achieved through investing. By aligning your future goals with the right types of investments, you will be able to plan for economic freedom and set yourself apart from the rest of the population who are relying on a meagre monthly income.

The moment you put your money in any asset, you are prepared for two eventualities; your asset will grow or depreciate over time. This change in value is influenced by economic, social and political factors.

It is tough to explain the market movements at onset until a pattern is developed. Market fluctuations are normal, though sometimes it is theatrical. It's difficult to make a decision while such variations occur, just as it is hard to navigate the desert during a sandstorm. It is important that you employ patience and make decisions when the dust has eventually settled.

Perhaps you have heard about timing the market in buying or selling assets for profit. But this is easier said than done. In the investment market, it's 'time' in the market, not 'timing' the market that counts, which makes a lot more sense.

The aim of this guide was to give you a basic understanding of the risks and rewards associated with investing, along with some basic pointers on strategy.

There are countless advanced strategy guides and schemes out there, some legitimate, some just out to take your money and run.

Before your dive into any investments, consider the points in this book carefully, in particular, your own goals.

Once you have established your 'why' you can begin to build your plan around that, with expert guidance along the way.

To minimize the risk of making mistakes early on, I have included a free bonus guide with this book. See the back page to get your copy now.